THE MAASAI

CULTURE. BELIEFS. EDUCATION

Lemomo Ole Kulet

THE MAASAI

Copyright © 2018 by Lemomo Ole Kulet

ISBN 9781980810018

Printed in USA

Dedication

This book is dedicated to my little daughter Nicole Siranka Kulet and all the people worldwide with an interest on Maasai culture, beliefs and education.

Also, to the future generations of Maa community who might not get a chance of experiencing the lifestyle of their forefathers.

Finally, to Sinore, Lyn, Mateu, Tubula, Nosim and Leshan.

Table of Contents

Foreword

The Maa Nation is renowned for resisting change. Save for insignificant variations, their culture has remained unchanged from time immemorial. The early explorers, missionaries and the first colonial administrators who had an encounter with the Maasai described them as fierce, arrogant, proud and valorous but adamantly attached to their way of life.

From the stories that were told by those who had an encounter with them, the world learnt that the Maa morans fought gallantly and conquered vast territories by driving inhabitants of such lands out of their habitations. However, it is known that they did not hold any territory they did not need for grazing their livestock. It is also known that in pursuit of their nomadic lifestyle, they were always on the move looking for rich green pastures. And because of their total dependence on livestock for sustenance, their lives always revolved around the management of these animals to the exclusion of any other life-sustaining activity. Consequently, their stories, their songs and even their thoughts were always about their livestock.

The belief that all the cattle were given to the founder of Maa by God has dominated their lives ever since. It is believed that, that could be the reason why they viciously raided all other cattle-owning people with an intention of herding back all cattle in those faraway lands to where they believed they rightly belonged. Being the center of gravity for the Maa people, cattle took center stage in the socio-economic and political activities of the nation.

The up-bringing of children, their early education and the training of the youth were all geared to and aimed at the envisaged life-long activities that centered on animal husbandry. It is little wonder therefore that matters to do with grazing lands, water and the security of the people and livestock were always given priority whenever matters concerning the welfare of the people were debated at the elders' councils.

Although, the Maasai were valorous and fought their adversaries gallantly and decisively, winning most of the wars, there were enemies that proved to be too strong for them. Some of those adversaries had dogged them from time immemorial and were instrumental to keeping their population low. The most crucial one was of their own making. For no apparent reasons morans of one section of the Maasai feuded against and picked quarrels with the rest of the sections' morans. Suddenly war broke out and the feuding morans faced off with the combined armies of the rest of the morans.

Predictably they were defeated, vanquished and annihilated. The same fate awaited other sections' morans who likewise arrogantly faced off with the combined strength of the rest of the sections' morans. They were too wiped off the face of the earth. Inevitably those senseless inter- sectional wars kept the Maa population low. The other enemies that were equally devastating were famine, drought and diseases. These natural disasters, especially the ones that hit Maasailand in 1889 nearly annihilated the Maa people and their cattle. These calamities brought temporary changes in the way the Maa people lived, sending most of them to neighboring communities begging for food. But because of their resilience, once the problem was over, they were able to bounce back and got back to living their lives once again as they lived before.

There are however insidious but subtle agents of change that have silently worked from within the people to bring out changes that are now changing the Maa culture albeit with some subtlety. There is the school education that has effectively interrupted moranhood and rendered it meaningless and irrelevant as far as cattle raids are concerned. Currently it is fighting to eradicate female genital mutilation the success of which will emancipate women. Christianity has too played a big role in dulling the force of culture over the community. But the straw that has broken the camel's back has been the change in the land tenure.

From time immemorial Maasai land had been communally owned. But in the advent of the change in land tenure which resulted in the land being individually owned, great change accompanied it. Changes came in the manner the new individualized land is managed. Nomadism is coming to an end and pastoral life has taken a new meaning. The place men and women occupied in the land that was communally owned has of necessity changed. Now each individual makes a decision that he/she deems appropriate without recourse to anybody else.

These are the changes that drove Jackson Lemomo Ole Kulet, the author of this book want to critically look at what the culture of the Maa people has been and compare it with the hybrid kind that is inevitably emerging. It will not escape the readers' eye that Lemomo has taken time to interview many elders who still remember what the unadulterated culture looked like. The findings that he gathered from the elders are invaluable and indeed they will become part of the history that will eventually be written while tracing the turbulent path the Maa have trodden to arrive at their present destination.

Dr. Nchorrira Naikuni, PhD
Lecturer
School of Business and Economics
Maasai Mara University

Acknowledgement

My sincere gratitude and thanks to *En-kai Magilani* for the grace and favour that has enabled me to finish this project successfully.

To my father's JohnMark Kamakei Kulet and Henry Rufus Ole Kulet thank you so much for the invaluable information you shared with me on Maasai way of life based on real life experience. My eldest dad H.R. Ole Kulet you have been a mentor and a source of inspiration on all aspects of life. Your literary work has inspired me a lot to write. We may not have had the opportunity to experience our way of life as exclusively as you did but we shall forever be grateful for having taught us the way of our forefathers.

To Nicholas Asego I am grateful for having been a great mentor and teacher on how to write. John Oywa thank you for your mentaship.

To the Standard Media who through their Kikwetu feature gave me an opportunity to write on Maa culture. Most of the articles in this book were first published by The

County Weekly a publication of The Standard Group Limited.

To my best friend and mentor Julius Sigei for insisting that I write and encouraging me all through the period I was writing.

To Charles Ng'eno my fellow scribe thank you for having read all that I ever wrote in The County Weekly.

To my brother and friend Frank Ole Kibelekenya thank you for your insights on this work and for having held my hand and supported me on many ways.

Rempeyian Murasmi and my younger brother Dr. Nchorrira Naikuni, thank you for your insightful contribution to this work.

To all my colleagues at Barclays Bank of Kenya; Nakuru East, Kabarnet and Narok branches I am sincerely grateful for making my work life good which in turn left mind with the right mind to write.

To Naneu my best friend and wife thank you for having been the first to proof read all the articles and for having typed most of them.

To all my readers during the period I was writing for the The County Weekly your persistent request that I combine all the articles into one book for the sake of posterity I say thank you a million times because your request is now a reality.

Finally, to all those I might have not mentioned here but in one way or another you supported my work I say *Ashe Oleng'*.

Author

Lemomo Ole Kulet is a strategic management specialist, banker and a writer with interest in culture, science, medicine and poetry.

Born in 1976 in Narok and raised in Nakuru. He is a holder of an MBA and currently pursuing his PhD in strategic management at the Jomo Kenyatta University of Agriculture and Technology.

Chapter One

RITUALS IN THE LIFE-CYCLE OF A MAASAI MAN

Great celebration and joyful singing from the women always greeted the birth of a baby boy among the Maasai community. It is here at birth, known in Maa as *E-inoto* that the life of a Maasai man begins.

Three to six months or four to six years (depending on the family) after the birth of the baby boy its head hair was shaved off together with that of its mother in a process known as *Aitupuku enkerai tiaji*.

This process would be followed by the naming ceremony known as *Orkipoket* in Maa. It is here that the child is given its proper name.

Mzee Jonah Ole Kasura notes that, "Due to high child mortality rate no one was sure of the child's survival hence new born were always given a pet name and for some time they would be called by the pet name. Once it was certain that the child would survive then a naming ceremony would be organized in order to give the new born a proper name"

During this ceremony a sheep would be slaughtered on the *Olmisigiyoi* (Rhus natalensis) or *Oloiren* (Oleo europaea) leaves and it would be roasted. This meat was called *Enaikwiti* and was only eaten by women. Once this was done a ceremony known as *En-kidungoto e nk-arna,* the cutting or the giving of a name was ready to be done.

I ask Mzee John Kamakei of Olchurai Gilgil why *Olmisigiyoi* and *Oloiren*? He tells me, "They are sacred and ceremonial trees. In almost all-important ceremonies these two trees play a critical part."

At this point David Sadera explains, "Two women and two elders would drink the beer, bless the child and then give it a new name to replace the nickname which it had up till then. It is now considered strong enough to survive."

Boyhood which is known as *Ayiokisho* is the stage where the boy grows up and learns to go out and graze the cattle in the company of other boys, both older and younger than himself.

E-murata which is the circumcision is divided into two unlike in the women where there is only one group to be circumcised. The two groups were made in order to ensure that there was a proper succession and training. Here we have *e-murata e tatene*, the circumcision of the right-hand resulting into the *ol-porror le dukuya*, the first circumcision-group, also known as *ol-porror botor,* the senior circumcision-group and e-*murata   e kedianye, the* circumcision of the left-hand resulting into the *ol-porror le siadi,* the second circumcision-group, also known as *ol-porror oti,* the junior circumcision-group.

E-murrano warrior hood, the institution of moranism originated from the need to have an army to handle cases of emergencies. It was intended to be a defense force against any invading enemy. The morans had a noble duty of being the custodians of both property and life. As the army of the community the code of conduct was strictly observed as in the convectional discipline forces. The purpose of the camp *(Emanyatta)* is to keep men of the same age set together and fulfil their role as a military force. This is where the warriors learn about the age set brotherhood, the art of oratory skills and animal husbandry. They will spend up to ten years in the *emanyatta* before the *Eunoto* ceremony (senior's warrior initiation).

Normally when the elders felt that the warriors had now served their years well, they would decide that it was now time for another set of young men to take over from the current ones and they would organize a special ceremony called *Eunoto. E-unoto* means establishing. This was a promotion ceremony for the junior warriors to the status of senior warrior, *ol-morijoi* and is by far the best known, most colourful and remarkable of all ceremonies in the life of the Maasai community. Its preparations are detailed and take a long time, including the construction of an *e-manyatta.*

Mzee Kasura notes that, "Maasai ceremonies are very symbolic. *Eunoto* for instance, since the morans have always have been on the move and taking responsibility belonging to the entire community and now they are being established from group responsibility of defence to individual responsibility."

The *Eunoto* ceremony was performed by members of the age set, ten years after warrior hood. It marked the status of a warrior transitioning to a senior warrior. This initiation also permits senior warriors to marry, which in turn prepares them to become future fathers.

Novelist H.R. Ole Kulet tells me that, *"Ol-ngesher* which means grid or meat-grill was another symbolic ceremony among the Maasai that come after *Eunoto*; it was a ceremony whereby warriors officially left warrior hood and become junior elders. It is symbolic in that during moranism they roasted meat using sticks and pegs of *Oloiren* tree but now that they are established at a homestead, they will be roasting meat using a grid or a meat grill."

The ceremony was marked by the drinking of milk, and the eating of meat; this went together with the *en-dungoto e n-keene;* the cutting of the rope, which signified the end of *en-turuj.*
Rimpeyian Murasimi explains; "*En-turuj* means taboo. As morans they had things that were a taboo for them to do. For instance, they could not drink milk or eat meat in the presence or in view of women. That's why they eat their meat in the forests away from the sight of women."

This he tells me; "Was geared towards preventing a Delilah-Samson scenario as they were the defenders of the community. They had to stay away from any manipulations from women. So, during the cutting of the rope at the *Ol-ngesher* ceremony; all these restrictions or taboos were removed allowing morans to participate in things they were not allowed during moranism."

The men then enter into *Payianisho*, elder hood. Here Robert Ole Masikonte of Enaibelibel location in Narok explains that as an elder he will observe a number of ceremonies. Such ceremonies include *ol-kiteng loo lbaa*, the ox of the wounds; this was a cleansing ceremony where by elders of the same age set - *Olporror* would come together and slaughter an ox in order to repent all the sins they did during their term as morans. It was basically cleaning themselves from the wounds of the past so as to bring peace in their old age.

He continues; "Other ceremonies included *o-lamal*, the delegation, *e-murata oo nkera*, the circumcision of his children, and attending *em-polosare oo nkera*, a sacrifice for his children whereby he would slaughter an ox as a sacrifice in dedication of his children to *Enk-ai* in presence of elders of his age set and *Oloibon*."

On a regular basis he will attend *en-kiguena*, the council of elders, and in time become a member of *ol-piron*; an important duty where the senior elders who are members of the *ol-piron* impart cultural instructions and education to the junior elders. He would during his free time visit other homesteads belonging to friends that they had been circumcised together.

Slowly but surely, he moves into *e-moruao*, old age ending up as *kakuyiaa*, grandfather. He will be a great source of wisdom and would really be close to his grandchildren to whom he would be a source knowledge given through stories.

En-keeya- death will ultimately follow and once he is dead, he would be laid out in the open, *en-kirragata,* folded away in a skin some distance from the homestead.

Unlike in the case of women whose life ends with their death; the Maasai man *En-jungore-* inheritance followed soon after mourning period, his sons together with the elders would control the inheritance.

Chapter Two

RITUALS IN THE LIFE-CYCLE OF A MAASAI WOMAN

The life of a Maasai woman begins by birth known as *E-inoto.* The birth of a girl like that of a boy to a Maasai family is normally greeted by a lot of Ululation from the women in order celebrate the good news and share in the family's happiness. A girl is so important to the Maasai as she is the hoard of fertility worth and the hope of continuity. In the Maa community women are the custodian of culture as they perpetuate it through activities as storytelling.

Rempeyian Murasimi notes that "When a child is born it is given a pet name and for some time the child would be called by the pet name. The pet name was given as child mortality rate was high and they

were not sure of the child's survival."
Examples of such pet names he tells me
included Nanana,Titi,Kerai just to mention
but a few. At this stage the mother retains
her hair known as *Ol-masi*. She does not
shave it. In fact, Jonah Ole Kasura an
elder from Ilmasheriani says "She does not
even take a bath during this period of
lactation. The intention was to make her
undesirable as long as she had a young
one to care for."

Ole Kasura continues, "Certain herbs are
burnt into fine soot that is diluted in
sheep fat and is used to smear her cloths.
Since she does not take bath or clean her
cloth during this period, she develops a
body odour that makes her undesirable."
This state of undesirability, he tells me, is
known as *Kerere*-someone who is dirty,
which effectively becomes a male repellent
and therefore acts as a family planning
method.

I inquired from novelist H.R.Ole Kulet whether this culture is still practiced to which he emphatically says yes. He says, "Certainly yes, this is a very important tenet in the Maa culture and it's very much practiced to date with an exemption of those who have embraced modernity." Ole Kulet explains that on the day she shaves the *Ol-masi* and discards the smelly cloths, cleans herself and puts on clean sheet, the husbands becomes aware that she is ready to conceive another child.

Some families would have the mother retain the hair until the child was given a proper name, other families because they give the proper name after a long period say four to six years would allow the mother to shave her hair while the child is growing. This practice either by design or default helped the Maasai to achieve family planning and may be explains why the Maasai though practicing polygamy are not numerous as expected. By the time another child was born, the earlier child was big enough to walk long distance. This ensured that children were not an impediment during periodic movement in the Maa nomadic life.

After three to six months or four to six years (depending on the family) after the birth of the girl its head hair is shaved off together with that of its mother in a process known as *Aitupuku enkerai tiaji*. Then a process known as *En-kidungoto e nk-arna:* the cutting or the giving of the name; the baby is given a proper name to replace the nickname it had up until then as the baby is now considered likely to survive. Before this the child is normally given a nickname known as *em-bolet* which is normally given to children at birth before they receive their proper name. The name is also known as *enk-*

arna e muro; the name of the hind leg. The proper name given to a child at *Em-barnoto e nkerai* is known as *enk-arna e ncorio* meaning the name of the front leg.

En-titoisho-girlhood or maidenhood is the stage where the little girl stays at home, progressively learning to look after the goat kids and lambs which graze around the *Enk-ang* or homestead. She helps her mother to tend the younger children and also help in some household duties. As she grows up, she is taught by the older women how to establish her own home and will accompany other girls and women to draw water from a nearby stream and collect firewood.

E-murata-circumcision, clitoridectomy; this ceremony is performed within the privacy of her mother's house. This practice is deeply entrenched in the Maasai customs and traditions. Sopia

Nolturesh, an old circumciser who has been in the business of circumcising girls for nearly thirty years tells me, "Circumcision of girls is as old as Maasinta (the legendary founding father of all the Maasai). This culture was with us when we ascended the Kerio Valley. Although you people say we should not circumcise girls, it's against Maa culture not to do so." She continues, "It's certainly a rite of passage and uncircumcised girl remains a child and cannot be married."

Maasai's are brought up trusting that uncircumcised girl-*entito neme murata*-is incomplete. Long time ago you would hardly find any uncircumcised girl but when Christianity came to Maasai land some families embraced it and dropped the idea of circumcising girls. This is where stigmatization begun. The stigmatization and possible social isolation of girls on grounds of being uncircumcised has forced many young Maasai girls to go for circumcision voluntarily. Most of the parents will never let their sons associate with uncircumcised girls let alone marrying them. This threat of stigmatization is much more tormenting than the practice itself. This explains why it's probably difficult to eradicate this barbaric custom. After *e-murata* the girl becomes *E-siankiki*. This is where the girl awaits her husband to be who had engaged her any time between childhood and the stage in which she is now. As soon as the spouse to be arrives she is shaved and she is taken away as a young bride.

After marriage the young woman, *e-siankiki*, will hopefully soon conceive and become an *en-tomononi*, mother. All the way through the years she will pray to God for many children and becomes *ngoto in-kera*, the mother of children.

Slowly by slowly she becomes *enk-kaputani*-mother in law then *en-tasat*, old lady, and finally *kokoo*, grandmother, a powerful force behind the scenes in the *enk-ang* and a spoiler of her loving grandchildren.

En-keeya-death will eventually come gently as she sleeps on her bed and she will be laid out in the open, *en-kirragata.*

Chapter Three

SPECIAL WOMEN AMONG THE MAASAI

Maasai women have and continue to play many important cultural roles in their communities. The most important of them all is that they have been the custodian of the Maasai culture. They are teachers who are highly respected in the Maa society and their opinion in important matters affecting the society was always appreciated contrary to the stereotype's belief held by many outsiders. Among these women of the Maa community, there exists some who are treated as special women. These women play different roles that make them stand out among the rest of the womenfolk. Some play positive roles while others play seemingly negative ones.

These women include the great *Enk-aitoyioni* –the midwife who is the traditional birth attendant, the *Enk-amuratani*-the circumciser whose role of circumcising girls is slowly coming to an end due to the campaign mounted to fight its retrogressive nature of the Female Genital Mutilation, *Entito e nkang'* –this is the girl-turned son or daughter of the home. These three group of women have special roles that are positive to the advancement of the Maa culture.

There is another set of special women that play rather negative roles in the Maasai community. They include the feared witch or sorceress the *Enk-asakutoni,* the divorcee who is known as the returnee one- *Enk-anyakuai,* and finally you have the undisciplined *En-taapai,* who becomes pregnant before she is circumcised.

The *Enk-aitoyioni* who is the traditional birth attendant and a midwife played and still plays a vital role in the community. She is the one who cared for the expectant mother. She takes charge of both the pre-natal and post-natal care of the pregnant women among the community.

Susan Seenoi notes, "She advices on healthy and careful eating during the pregnancy. She has special knowledge of types of foods to be eaten by expectant mothers during this period. She also knows various types of herbs that pregnant women would use to boost their blood levels and also purify their blood system for healthy living."

She is the one who will assist in the delivery of the child. And when the baby delivered from the womb, it is her who will receive the baby into her hands. Her most important duty during delivery is to safely sever the umbilical cord.

The *Enk-amuratani* even though her role is slowly being phased out due to worldwide campaign against FGM, she continues to be an important figure in the community especially in molding and teaching the young girls.

Robert Ole Masikonte says, "Unlike the Maasai men who are circumcised by the *Iltorobo* tribes' men who only did the physical part and went away, the *Enk-amuratani* would go further to teach the circumcised girls their expectations in the larger society. She would teach them what entails their chores, the importance of not being adulterous. She would also inculcate the art of hard work in them."

We have the girl-turned son, or the daughter of the home- *Entito e nkang'*. A man may choose to keep a daughter at home, rather than have her married, if he has no male descendants. In this way he acquires male descendants through the children that his daughter bears. There are scenarios, though rare, whereby a father may have fathered only girls. In such a situation the old man is expected to prevail upon one of his daughters from getting married. The young woman was then authorized to have children at her father's home with any man of her choice. When she gets a baby boy then it was pronounced the heir of the old man's property.

Enk-asakutoni- is the witch, the sorceress. She is greatly feared for her black magic. She is believed to have the power to contact the spirits. Everyone fears to be pointed by her. It is a taboo to point one's finger at someone among the Maasai as it is seen as a form of bewitching and certainly so when it is done by the *Enk-asakutoni.*

Purity Nooseuri tells me, "When a group of women are competing among themselves some would go and consult the *Enk-asakutoni* with the aim of bewitching their rivals. In such a scenario, the bewitched one may also consult another *Enk-asakutoni,* and in that case it becomes a rivalry of witches."

Enk-anyakua is the returnee. She is the woman or wife who has returned to her father's homestead after having been married and bride price paid. Such a woman is derided and scorned as a worthless baggage to her father.

En-taapai is the girl who becomes pregnant before circumcision known as a seduced one. The child she gets out of this is known as *Enkerai-e-ntapaai* – a child of seduction who is considered to be an illegitimate child. When girls get into this unfortunate situation, she is regarded as 'soiled goods' and no young man would want to marry her. In fact, she was usually circumcised at the time of child birth. When she was healed, she was married off to the oldest man in the village. Subsequently, the Maasai teenagers are taught to refrain from improper sexual behaviors particularly to avoid pregnancy before marriage. In fact, it is a taboo for an uncircumcised female or male to have children. Girls are even made to wear deterrent anklets symbolic of preventing unwanted pregnancies.

Chapter Four

DUTIES OF A MAASAI WOMAN

The Maasai woman plays an important role in the day to day affairs of her home and the wider community. Being the person nature has given the role of nurturing children; she is inevitably the custodian of the Maasai culture and therefore ensures continuity of the Maasai traditions.

Her role in the society complements that of the Maasai man. She does much more physical work than the man, her chores are rather repetitive while those of the man are Managerial in nature and often require decision making.

While the Maasai men are tasked with a fundamental responsibility of running the affairs of their society. Women are culturally expected to do many chores which include constructing their huts, fetching water, gathering firewood, milking cattle, cooking, bringing up of children and keeping the household in a functioning manner. She also has a role of coaching young girls into young adults, mothers and future role models.

Men do less of the physical work than women but they ensure that the entire village runs and functions smoothly. Their main responsibilities include building the fence around the enk-ajijik or the enk-ang', to protect the entire village from predators, external aggressors, and herding large livestock.

Each Maasai woman lives in her own house and she is responsible for her family and properties including livestock. She makes decisions that are related to her family unit while leaving the major decisions affecting the wider family to the man.

Although she does not own any property since all the properties including cattle belong to her husband, her husband apportions a number of cows, sheep and goats to her from which she takes charge of the products such as milk, butter, meat, hide/skin etc. She can sell the milk and other products and her husband would never ask for any proceeds from such sale.

As mentioned herein above, one of the major roles of a Maasai woman is to construct her house. She does this often by the assistance of her colleagues.

Sopia Nookipa explains, "When it comes to building the house, one gets assistance from her colleagues. It is one of those roles that are one off and hence we assist each other in the construction of the house"

The house consists of poles erected in a rectangular manner with round corners. Twigs are placed in between the poles to fill the gaps. It is then plastered with mud and cow dung mixture. The roof is flat or really so and consists of branches supported by peripheral poles. They are small and windowless hunt with the only opening a small one being made in order to act as a chimney which enables smoke escape from the hut.

A day in the life of a Maasai woman is full of activities. She wakes up at around 5.30am

Jerusha Naneu says, "We wake up very early in the morning in order to milk the cows and goats. We also have to monitor and report to our husband any sick or pregnant cows"

After milking the cows, the women would then proceed to make breakfast for their entire family. This would be milk, tea and in some cases porridge.

Once everyone has taken their breakfast and the men have already taken the cattle to graze the women would embark on other important chores of the day like fetching of fire wood and water. The whole process of gathering, fetching and bringing firewood and water home may takes up the better part of their day light time, sometimes up to two-third of the entire day.

Seleina Nkadayo notes, "We travel many kilometers averagely six to seven kilometers every time we go to fetch, either firewood or water. It is a journey fraught with danger. Elephants, buffaloes, lions, snakes and many other dangerous animals are what we encounter every time we fetch water and firewood. It is dangerous activity but we have no option as we have a noble responsibility to fulfill."

Occasionally wild animals, especially elephants would trample on an unfortunate woman killing her before burring her in a heap of tree branches' bringing untold suddenness to the entire community. Once this happens men would arm themselves, and go to the forest to avenge the dead woman by killing the marauding elephant.

On arrival from collection of firewood and water they would then clean the home and make lunch for her children. Lunch is rare among the Maasai families as there are generally two meals a day, one in the morning and one at night

Pauline Siloma says, "Once we have made lunch for our family then it's time to engage in bead work. Maasai women are creative and they like designing new ornamental artifacts every time they get that opportunity. They do this for their husbands, children and also for commercial purposes."

In the evening she must make fire before everyone comes back. She has to bring in calves and goat kids into the enclosures.

Then she has to milk the cows again and prepare more food for the entire family including any visitors.

Joan Nashipai says, "With this kind of culture we never get bored. Our day is fully packed and we are happy."

Maasai women have some other roles which include participating in organizing, singing and serving everyone at ceremonial occasions. Once in a while the women would congregate and organize themselves into delegations that would go for prayer for a specific purpose such as prayers to have babies; known in Maasai as Enk-ai aomon entomono or prayers to God to bring to an end an epidemic. At 10pm they would go to bed to sleep after others are already asleep.

Chapter Five

MAASAI EDUCATION

Education is a very important tool to any community as it guarantees continuity. Among the Maasai cultural education was given a greater importance and priority. The goal of the Maasai education was to maintain a cohesive society, ensure survival of the migratory lifestyle and learn the tasks related to the various roles within the community.

Although modern day Maasai children go to school to receive formal education they are also socialized with the tribe's values of collective ideology, cohesion, respect for elders and conformity to the tribe's norms and rituals. They are also taught everything about cattle tending, health care and the defense of the people. The teaching is accomplished through direct observation, participation and apprenticeship of all oral traditions of the Maasai.

The Maa community conducted training by imparting acquired knowledge and experiences gained by elders through the medium of indigenous knowledge passed down from one generation to the other from time immemorial.

According to Mwalimu Frank Ole Kibelekenya the Maa education was meant to enable recipients cope up with their environment and ascertain their survival. This form of education he says was a way through which important attributes, values, skills and attitudes were transferred from elders to the younger generation in order for them to function as per the expectation.

For both girls and boy's education was taken very seriously. For the girl's intensive education on their culture and expectations was given to them before marriage. During *e-murata* - circumcision which was performed within the privacy of her mother's house the girl was taken through intensive training on her roles and responsibilities. These teachings were done by the circumciser.

As for the boys during and after circumcision the training was less intensive. Mzee Robert Ole Masikonte of Enaibalibel explains; "That was because boys were normally circumcised by the *Iltorobo* men, who were not expected to teach the Maasai boys anything, for they did not belong to the Maa community".

After recuperation the newly, circumcised Maasai boys would go to the institution of morranism. It was in this military like barracks that a comprehensive indigenous teaching and learning took place for the boys, imparted to them by elders.

The all-encompassing training was tailored towards the inculcation of the deep-rooted values of the Maasai pastoral and nomadic life. Here the learning and training was meant to impart important skills for living and survival. This training took six or seven years with the sole aim of imparting knowledge to the young men on their physical environment, social-cultural activities and civic education.

Rimpeyian Murasimi notes that the syllabus of the Maasai education was varied and wide. It ranged from civic education, military studies, social and family life studies, environmental and economic studies. Animal husbandry was also an integral part of this syllabus.

Defense was critical to the Maasai community and that's why military training was part of morranism. It was here that the Morans were taught the art of war-theory and practice of warfare. Several war strategies were taught to prepare the young men in their role of defending their people from external attack. It was in this training where the highest form of discipline was inculcated into the Morans.

The other education that took place was about understanding the environment- the study of the flora and fauna. Here herbalist Konene Ole Turere notes that the young men were taught the importance of the environment to the survival of the

Maasai community. The young men learn about plants and animals various land features and their relevance to the life of a Maasai. It was that kind of Maasai education that enabled the Maasai community to co-exists harmoniously with their environment.

It's here that the young men were taught the curative properties of various shrubs, trees and tubers that were used for the health of both humans and animals. They were taught various types of diseases in both humans and animals and their remedies. They were taught which plants were capable of curing certain diseases.

During Morranism wealth creation was also taught. The young men were taught skills and attitudes that would enhance the acquisition of cattle and management of livestock.　This was where raids to acquire cattle were taught.

On social and family life studies the young men were taught the value of social cohesion, comradeship which was very important during and after Morranship, ceremonies and ritual of the Maa community were also taught here, importance of corporate unity was also taught.

Family life gender relations and marital responsibilities were also taught. Family responsibility that included marriage, inheritance and social strata were taught. Civic education was also a critical area where the emphasis was on patriotism, love for the society and obedience to the leaders.

Chapter Six

GROOMING, DECORATION AND BODY PIERCING AMONG THE MAASAI

The Maasai culture encouraged competitiveness among its young people based on the natural attributes of their bodies. For instance, a young man or woman endowed with milk-white teeth planted on black gums, a girl who in addition to these had a natural gap between her upper front teeth called *enchilaloi*, or a handsome tall lanky young man with a natural springy gait, were always admired by many and given preferential treatment during festivals and other occasions. However, these natural endowments were not regarded as sufficient attraction. Over the years culture evolved and developed and, in the process, defined aesthetics to enhance the desired attractiveness. These in turn became mark of identity and beauty. And each young man, each young woman would go to any length, endure whatever pain in order to attain the additional attractiveness. These additional attainments of the desired impression came in stages and along with an acute pain that had to be stoically endured.

Removal of the Lower Jaw Front Teeth

The first of the many painful operations done to enhance the desired attractiveness was the removal of the two lower front teeth. It is called *aboe*. According to Nicole Noonkiyiaa, although the need to remove the two teeth was necessitated by occasion of lock jaws in the past due to diseases, and the gap was used to pass liquid into the locked jaws, the gap was said to enhance beauty and handsomeness. The teeth were removed when a child was young as three years of age.

Piercing of the Upper Part of the Ear

The process is called *Aud-imaroro*. It is a painful operation done to boys and girls aged six. A red-hot needle is used to pierce a hole on the upper part of each ear. A slender stick is put into the created hole and every now and then turned around to ensure the hole made is maintained. When healed, the holes are used to hang bead ornaments called *muna*. Peter Koiyiara notes; "This is a very painful operation but again the child is encouraged to endure the pain for the sake of future beauty and decorations called *Enkuso* or *Enkodo*."

Piercing of the Earlobes

Robert Ole Masikonte of Enaibelbeli location in Narok County says; "Between the age of 12 and 13, both boys and girls undergo another painful process known as *Aud-Inkiyaa*. This is the curving out of a circular hole in each ear-lobe using a sharp knife. A round piece of wood known as *Enkulale* shaped to fit into the created hole in the earlobe is inserted." Often the wound gets infected and takes a long time to heal. However, when healed, the young men and women would proudly show off the bead-ornaments that are hung on there. Later in life he notes, men would adorn ear-rings called *Ilmintoni* while old women would hang bead-decorated ornaments called *Inkonito-o-Nkiyaa* or scrolled copper ear-rings known as *isurutia.*

Creating Decorative Scars

At the age of 10-12, boys and girls would create decorative scars known as *Ilkipirat*. They would do this by placing a burning bud of dry Oleleshua leaves on their thighs and fore-arms and they would persevere and endure the entailed pain as the burning bud created a circular wound on the skin. Ten of such circular scars in two parallel lines on the thighs and fore-arms ensued after the wounds healed. They were said to be decorative and they enhanced beauty.

Writings on the Skin

This was the most beautiful decoration that was meant for the Morans only. It was called *Aiger* or *Apik Ilkigerot*. Novelist H.R. Ole Kulet notes; "A sharp object was used to make nicks on the body, in a pre-determined pattern, usually two parallel lines that started on each breast and went down to the stomach. The Moran who had these decorative scars was called *Oloigero*-the one with writings on his body." Interestingly when the art of writing was introduced by the Europeans, it was this form of decorative art that provided the verb *Aiger*, meaning to write in Maasai.

Grooming

There is nothing that the young Maasai men and young women cherish more than praises heaped on each of them based on their enhanced beauty, handsomeness or outstanding performance. They would take time and endure pain in order to attain these. Two Morans, for instance, would take many hours plaiting one another's hair. And women would sit for days making bead-ornaments. Even physical pain would not deter the young people from attaining the desired looks. This is the reason why words such as *Enkuso*, which means smartening up or *Enkodo* which means decoration by way of adornment, are always in each young person's lips. *Engiria*, which means to endure, embraces the virtues of perseverance. All these make grooming up for the purpose of presenting oneself as the most handsome or beautiful young person, the driving force that brings to fore the most cherished virtues of endurance, perseverance, bravely and valour.

Chapter Seven

THE MAASAI MARRIAGE AND THE SPEAR PLANTING MYTH

Marriage known in Maa as *En-kiyama* is a culmination of a very noble process. This process can be in two forms. First, two families may like each other so much and when either of the women; of the of the two families becomes pregnant the other family would visit their counter parts and with either butter or cow-dung of which they will use to mark the belly of the pregnant woman a process known as *E-siret e nk-oshoke*– the marking of the womb. This is an engagement already. So should the woman give birth to a baby girl the other family will provide the boy who will marry this young girl when time is ripe. In case the child happens to be a baby boy the other family will provide a girl who will hence forth be married to the little boy. This is mostly found in those families that really desire to strengthen their relationships with each other and it's rarely practiced these days.

The other form which is most common among the Maasai according to Mzee Tiampati Ole Masikonte of Enaibelibel is a process that begins with a man meeting a girl that he grows to like. The man will go praising the lady known in Maa as *a-serem en-tito* and he will then go on to place a small chain known as *Ol-pisiai* on her. This news like bush fire will spread very fast and shortly after the prospective bridegroom will bring honey and give it to the women of his clan living in the girl's neighborhood. It's these women who will in turn take the honey and milk to the mother of the girl. This honey is also known as *E-siret e nk-oshoke*– in this case a 'sign of the stomach' since when a girl becomes engaged to a man a sign with butter or cow-dung is made on her belly as an indication of engagement.

Ole Masikonte notes that after sometime the young man will again bring some honey but this time the honey will be much more than the first time. It is again given to the women who this time will brew it in to honey-beer to be given to the men. This will include the father to the girl, his brothers, elders of his clan and elders of his circumcision group known as *Ol-porror*. When the beer is ready to be served, the young man's escort comes to talk with the elders about the prospective marriage. This beer is called – *En-Kiroret*- a thing to talk with, a drink over which to hold discussions.

Mzee Jonah Ole Kasura of ilmasheriani Narok explains "It's during these discussions that the man who had proposed is told whether his proposal is acceptable. If the parents agree then a lifelong friendship called *En-kaputi* is cemented immediately while on the other hand if his proposal is rejected, he is also informed."

Assuming that the proposal is acceptable Mzee Kasura notes "The bridegroom on the wedding day brings two heifers and one bull, all of which ought to be of the same colour and blameless with no scars. He also brings two female sheep, a ram and an ewe. Of the heifers brought by the young man one is given to the girl's father so that there after the young man and his father-in-law will call each other '*Pa-kiteng*' or '*En-tawuo*'while the lamb is given to the bridegroom's mother-in-law and henceforth the young man and his age set call her '*Pa-ker*' meaning the one whom I gave an ewe."

Such a marriage is highly regarded and a divorce is not envisaged. The woman is regarded as the first and paramount wife in that home. Being polygamous the Maasai men will marry more than one wife. All these wives will stay within one enclosure known as *En-kang' which* has several huts, one for each of the wives.

It's within these Enclosures that it has always been misconstrued that a man can enter an *En-kang'* and go straight to one of the huts 'plant' a spear and goes on to have the woman of the house for the night. This cultural phenomenon has over the years brewed some controversy and requires elucidation.

The myth of "planting a spear" has its origin probably in a misunderstood truth. According to the myth, all that a male visitor visiting a Maasai Village needs to do is plant his spear outside a woman's house, and she is his for the asking. It is true that a man could plant a spear outside a woman's house and befriend the woman of the housed and proceeds to partake the illicit love that is proffered, just as it would happen in any other society. But it would be disastrous to assume that any sojourner who finds accommodation in a woman's house automatically finds conjugal accommodation as well.

The truth of the matter according to a renowned novelist and the winner of the Jomo Kenyatta Prize for Literature, 2009 H.R. Ole Kulet is that in the Maasai Society, any sojourner is entitled to two forms of hospitality, namely, food to eat and a house to sleep in and let it be known that Maasai men travel a lot, crisscrossing the savannah lands in pursuit of various missions that include, finding pastures for their livestock, visiting relatives etc. in all these journeys they never carry food, nor do they ever sleep in the forests, for culture has provided for these needs.

Ole Kulet notes "the house in which a man finds accommodation is usually owned by a wife belonging to his circumcision age group. The husband is not allowed by culture to sleep in the same house with the sojourner. And since such an elder usually has more than one wife, he moves to his other wife, leaving the visitor to sleep in the house he first entered. It may be assumed that (if he is randy) the visitor may (and this is unlikely) woo the wife, but success or failure of such an adventure is a purely personal matter, and is never encouraged. It may also be pertinent to add that Maasai women don't give in easily. And a woman who is known to accept the lure of a sojourner is looked down upon and considered to be promiscuous".

But where did the question of "planting a spear" spring from? Ole Kulet explains "When a man is traveling, he always carries either a spear or a sword or both. At nightfall he stops in a home and asks for the house of his age-group, naming the particular age-group to which he belongs. The house is pointed out to him. He plants his spear at the entrance and he goes in to book his accommodation for the night. In every Maasai house there are two beds, the woman's bed, (commonly known as small bed) and the big bed, (known as the large bed). The visitor unties his sword and hangs it at a prominent place by the large bed as a sign that he has booked, **not the woman**, but the bed. Any other visitor arriving in the same house, by merely looking, will know that there is already a visiting male in the house and will therefore have to go out to look for accommodation elsewhere."

Adultery, especially across age-groups is never tolerated, and is completely prohibited. If detected, the persons involved are warned by an elder. A repeat is usually settled in a violent manner that serves as an unpalatable deterrent that discourages future attempts.

Chapter Eight

SPECIAL GROUPS AMONG THE MAASAI COMMUNITY

Among the Maasai there exist some distinctive groups which play a very important role in ensuring Maasai culture is upheld. They exist outside the sections and territorial divisions of the Maasai and hence more often referred to as occupational groups. They include three special groups namely the *ilkunono,* *Iltorobo* and the *iloibonok.* The *ilkunono* are feared a lot due to their secretive nature and their way of life, the *iltorobo* are scorned due to their poverty and the *iloibonok* are respected and revered due to their ritual expertise and herbal medicine knowledge.

Ilkunono the blacksmith forms large part of this group. They are treated as a dejected caste or underclass within the pastoral communities. In fact, to some sections of the Maasai such as the Purko marriage with the *ilkunono* was traditionally strictly prohibited but due to education things are now changing as it's now possible to find a Purko man marrying a daughter of the *ilkunono.*

Ilkunono are the blacksmith who are mostly found in Suswa, some parts of Morijo Loita and also in Narok town. You probably have seen them in our towns and local centres merchandizing their products which they have made. Occasionally you will find a Maasai man move from place to place with cow bells, belts, bangles, arrow heads, spears, and ornamental earrings for both men and women, every kind of swords that you may think of and also bracelets. These are the *ilkunono.*

Kiranto Maasinta notes; "They are feared among the Maasai community as they were seen as merchants of death by the mere fact that they made things like arrows, spears, swords and may other war fare equipments and weapons that could be used to kill."

He continues; "The activities of this group meant that other Maasai's treated them as "polluted". There was generally an impression of pollution attached to blacksmiths; their food and welcome was in most cases avoided. They were considered unclean and were positioned at the lowest stratum of the Maasai society."

Mzee Lesiamon Turanta says; "It is an extremely gifted section of the Maasai and they have a business acumen that no other group of the Maasai community could come close to. Unfortunately, most of the other groups of the Maasai do not recognize them at all with some like the Purko who did not even allow their kids to either marry or be married to the ilkunono. It was a taboo to marry from them majorly due to stereotyping."

Mzee Lemein observes that if this part of the Maa community would have been accorded necessary attention given their ability to innovate and their entrepreneurial spirit then the Maasai community would have undergone a kind of industrial revolution and ending up achieving financial independence which has been so elusive to date.

Ilkunono are a very secretive community and would not disclose their plans or schemes unlike other groups of the Maasai who rarely keep any secrets. They were also involved with black magic which made other groups to fear them even more. They were looked down upon since they did not have as many cows as the other sections of the Maasai, their major preoccupation being their blacksmith activities.

Among the Maasai a rich man was considered one with many cows and many wives to which the *ilkunono* could not fit. These preoccupation with raring of cattle has become very difficult and unsustainable due to erratic weather pattern, decimated grazing areas, diseases and many more environmental issues. But to the *ilkunono* there is no day that their products would not be required. They would always be in demand. Their business brings in a lot of money to them and it is ironical that in Suswa they are the most successive in all spheres of life.

The *iltorobo* are the other category that the Maasai looked down upon. The word *Iltorobo* is translated to mean poor people without cattle. They were not Maasai but lived close to them and spoke their language. They were actually hunters and gatherers. They occupied parts of the Loita forest and also the Mau forest. They lived on fruits, insects, honey and hunting. Among the Maasai it was traditionally a taboo to use wildlife as food. So, whoever hunted wildlife for food was equated to an *oltoroboni.*

Kiranto Lemein tells me; "They did the work that the Maasai abhorred doing. Such jobs like male circumcision and running errands was done by them. They also sold honey and ceremonial skins made of Hyrax and Columbus to the Maasai."

The *iltorobo* no longer roam in the forest have been largely been assimilated in to the Maasai and those in the Mau forest have been mostly assimilated among the Kipsigis while most have remained as Ogiek but they still retain their way of life.

The last group is the *iloibonok* the medicine men who are also ritual experts. They are a from a sub-clan known as *Inkidong'i* who are renowned as ritual experts and diviners. They are mostly found in Liota area of Narok County. Unlike the first two groups the *iloibonok* command great respect in the community. They are seers and are thought to have the power to predict calamities and also prescribe remedies. They have a huge social and spiritual responsibility.

Mzee Robert Ole Masikonte tells me; "They were always consulted during major ceremonies and events taking place among the Maa community; such as wars, promotions of age sets, cleansing ceremonies and other important ceremonies."

Due to their vast knowledge on medicinal plants they also did the preparation of medicine for the treatment of various ailments. Their tools of trade are comprised of; a collection of paraphernalia for healing, a gourd known as *enkidong'* which is normally used by the Laibons for predictions and herbs.

There are many Laibons but there is only one Chief Laibon a prestigious position. He presides over all important social events and ceremonies among the Maasai community. This position is normally inherited as not just anyone can be a Laibon. Once the Chief Laibon felt it was time to hand over the mantle he would select one of his sons to be his successor.

The greatest threat to this group so far is Christianity which has always condemned their activities of this group and they have managed to convert a few to Christianity.

Chapter Nine

POLYGAMY AND DIVORCE AMONG THE MAASAI

Polygamy was and still is a practice found in almost all African societies. It is the practice or custom of marrying more than one wife.

Among the Maasai polygamy is deeply entrenched. It is in the very heart of the Maasai cultural believes and traditions.

The kind of polygamy practiced by the Maasai is different from others in that it was not regarded as an acquisition of another wife to the husband per se, but an additional hand to lighten the domestic burden. Here the practice had several functions that were very much related to the core values among the Maasai community.

Miccleland Sankok explains that marrying a new wife did not in any way threaten the existing rights of the other co-wives. For instance, cattle from one wife were not taken to be given to the newly married one, rather the husband drew from his unallocated herd to give to the new wife.

All wives are treated equally by the husband. However, the first wife had a special seniority status accorded to her by the younger wives. They acknowledge her and, in some instances, refer to her as 'mother'.

Among the Maasai polygamy was more of benefit to the co-wives more than the husband. Culture mandated the women to help each other when one of them became incapacitated or over-whelmed by the daily chores.

The Maasai man would ideally marry once he had become an elder. In practice however he only married when he was economically stable and able to establish an independent household. Ability to marry an additional wife among the Maasai was viewed in terms of livestock that one had.

There are many reasons why the Maasai practice polygamy. Peter Koiyiara says; "It was due to several aspects which include increased number of livestock, prestige and suggestion from the first wife. Among the Maasai polygamy was and is closely tied to the economic status of the man. For any Maasai man to be wealthy he needed to have more wives for it was the wives and the children who took care of the cattle. To take care of large number of cattle one needed to have a large family which could only be achieved through polygamy".

The other reasons he notes had to do with acquisition of the prestigious status in the society. Any respected elder among the Maasai had to have a sizeable household.

Against the popular misconception that it was the men alone who made decision to marry more than one wife, the first wife among the Maasai could suggest to her husband to marry a second wife. This could be as a result of pressure of work on her part or due to the fact that she wished to see his status in the community rise.

An unmarried woman may also approach a wealthy man for marriage, since she needed to have a recognized status in the society. Marriage among the Maasai was and is still so sacred that not a single day divorce was envisaged, in fact among the Maasai there was no directly translated word for divorce.

Divorce was unheard among the Maa community. It was considered a very shameful thing, especially for the divorced woman and her father, hence the oldman would do everything in his ability to ensure his daughter remains with her husband. Such a woman was called *Enkanyakuai.*

Susan Noonkipa explains that divorce was made impossible due to various reasons which included; the strong relationship known as *enkaputi* that was established during the marriage process and developed between the two families, such a break-up would have consequences which are far greater than the individual couple since among the Maa marriage is a community affair and not an individual affair.

The fact that children among the Maasai belonged to the father's lineage made it difficult for any would be divorcee as she is not allowed to take the children away with her unless it was a breast-feeding child.

Mzee Johnah Kasura notes that the issue of paying back all or part of the bride price also made it hard for a couple to think of divorce. Even in a proven case of adultery by the wife, there was usually no divorce, rather, some fine was imposed on the guilty party, and the wife's father may bring a cow and beseech the husband to keep his daughter in order to ward off the great humiliation of her being divorced. This was considered full restoration and was almost universally preferred to breaking up the family unit.

For any formal dissolution of marriage, it required a meeting of elders to settle the issue, and because it implied the return of bride wealth, it would be an almost impossible thing for any father-in-law who is not so well off. If a divorce should nevertheless happen, then the situation would be very difficult.

The divorce would find it extremely difficult to be re-married and would be regarded as good for nothing whereby no man would want to have her as a wife. It would also be a great shame to the father of the woman.

Chapter Ten

CIRCUMCISION AND GROUP LEADERSHIP

From time immemorial, the Maa people had recognized the important role that leadership played in molding and galvanizing the community within its cultural structures. The founders had known that through experience that exemplary leadership in one given circumcision-group would usher in a period of prosperity, peace and tranquility during and after their warrior hood.

It was because of that recognition that a thorough vetting exercise was carried out by elders and peers before one was selected as a ritual or political leader of the Maa according to educationist Frank Ole Kibelekenya.

Each Maasai section (*Olosho*) had its own political and ritual leaders. Leaders were selected from an age-group as early as before the boys were circumcised.

Rimpeyian Murasimi notes that those selected during warrior hood (moranhood) retained their positions throughout their lives. At the end of the moranhood stage, the leaders' long hair was cut in sequence of their ranks, to become junior elders.

The following are some of the most important leadership positions that were created to offer leadership to the circumcision-group.

Olorripu Olkila who is the guardian of the cloak and who is normally chosen by the *Ilmakesen* clan does the collection of a small skin from each of the five clans among the Maa community. He then gives his mother to make a cloak from them.

Mzee Johana Ole Kasura explains that the cloak symbolizes the integrity of the entire Maa community and total inclusiveness.

Once the cloak is ready, it is given to the *Olopolosi Olkiteng* who is chosen from the *Ilmolelian* clan. The boy chosen as *Olopolosi Olkiteng* will take the cloak to the ceremonial settlement for the ceremony of catching the ox by the horn. It is here that the boys catch the ox and bring it down by its horns using bare hands. *Olopolosi Olkiteng* who is also known as the smother of the oxen is normally the leader of this particular ceremony.

Mzee Robert Ole Masikonte of Enaibelibel location in Narok county explains that the *Olopolosi Olkiteng* is chosen before the ceremony is performed and it is him who will carry all the age groups sins. Hence it is a position that is considered unfortunate since he has to shoulder all of this age groups sin.

Novelist H. R. Ole Kulet notes that since he is the donor of the ox to be offered as a sacrifice, he is cleansed from the past sins but he is expected to stay away from any future sins.

Olorrip Olasar known as the guardian of the sacrificial fire is one of the most important of the office bearers and is set to guard the sacrificial fire. He is chosen from the *Iltaarosero* clan. This became necessary according to Ole Kulet; after a leopard once stealthing got into the ceremonial manyatta when the boys were asleep and carried away the sacrificial meat and brought about bad omen to the circumcision-group. Even after the meat is roasted and eaten, he remains behind to guard the site of the ceremony until a delegation of elders and initiates go to escort him home where the women and girls meet him with songs and dances.

The smother of the ox uses the cloak to smother the ox where the horn is caught when the ceremony is held at the special settlement called *emanyatta e mowuo olkiteng.*

Olaigwanani - he is a young man selected on the basis of his conduct and behavior. He leads the rest of the circumcision-group by becoming the first to get involved in all ceremonial rituals. He becomes the first to be circumcised of his age-group and leads his age-mates through all ceremonies and rituals until old-age.

He is head of his group of morans and takes care of all matters at the morrans manyatta. He is the commander during wars.

After morans are retired Ole Kasura notes that his function will be to settle family disputes among his age-group. He remains *olaigwanani* for life.

Olotuno - he is the chief leader of the morans and he is considered to be a highly disciplined individual. He must not have any defects and must have lived an exemplary life. He must not have any blemishes, must not have murdered and must not carry any scars. He is selected during *eunoto* ritual when warriors graduate to become elders. He becomes the first to marry. He is superior in rank to the *olaigwenani.*

Oloburu enkeene- he is known as the cutter of the strap. He is elected at the *eunoto* ceremony. His role is very important as is symbolic. *Eunoto* was a ceremony whereby warriors officially left warrior hood and became junior elders.

Novelist H. R. Ole Kulet explains; "During moranism they roasted meat using sticks and pegs of O*loiren* tree but at *Ol-ngesher* they are established at a homestead and they will be roasting meat using a grid or a meat grill."

The ceremony was marked by drinking of milk, and the eating of meat; this went together with the *en-dungoto e n-keene*, the cutting of the rope, which signified the end of the *en-turuj* which are taboos in English. This cutting is done by the cutter of the strap.

Chapter Eleven

LEADERSHIP AND INTEGRITY AMONG THE MAASAI

Leadership among the Maasai is a very important issue that is given a lot of weight every time it is discussed. Known in Maa as *e-rikore* is sacrosanct. The authority of the leader was highly respected. No one would question the leader as he was viewed as the wisest of all. The process of selecting a leader was a rigorous one and it started as early in life as possible-before boys are circumcised.

Once the elders met and decided that the boys were ready to be circumcised a home was constructed in which the boys were going to dance and perform ritual known as *Enkipataa*. While the dance was going on the elders would be busy engaging in negotiations on who is going to be selected to be a leader of the boys to be circumcised.   A thorough vetting reminiscent of the chapter six of our constitution was embarked upon. All the boys were vetted and the one who was selected become the Chief Councillor known in Maasai as *Olaiguenani*. He was supposed to be more mature mentally more than the others, widely respected and his council was taken seriously by all. He was expected to be handsome, well-built and without any imperfection.

Once he was picked, he was given the club known as *Orinka* which has been blackened by being submersed in mud as a way of curing, and which became a sceptre of leadership. The young man chosen would lead all the rest throughout the process of circumcision.

After the circumcision again the elders would vet the warriors known as *Ilmurran* to elect a Chief Councillor. The

Olaiguenani will then be the leader of a particular *emanyatta.* This entire process of vetting by the elders was so secretive that no one ever knew who was going to be selected.

Every warrior dreaded being chosen as they knew the responsibility bestowed upon such a leader was immense. They knew too that the person chosen would lose the privileges that went with being carefree youth.

Once the elders felt that the group of morans have served their years as protectors of property and life in the community they organized for a takeover by another set of young warriors in a ceremony known as *Eunoto* (senior's warrior initiation). Again, at that stage, the elders would again select a warrior of high respect and reputation who is going to lead the way for others to be initiated into elder hood.

This selection was so secretive as the leader to be selected was rigorously vetted. He must be without a scar, he must not be left handed, not impotent, good natured and always even-tempered, more importantly he must not have committed murder. The bottom line was that he must be without blemish. The selected leaders' family was also scrutinized to ensure that his father and grandfather, were people of good character. The young man also had to be a good orator and listener, generous and polite.

Johnmark Kamakei of Olchurai tells me, "The vetting was so intense and very objective. Subjectivity was not tolerated at all. The elders would agree to disagree with intelligence and humility. The nominees to be vetted would be scrutinized thoroughly. At some point the debate would be so intense until it would go into a kind of committee's stage as would happen in our parliament. At this moment you will hear like-minded individuals telling each other *Emaape enkilepata* – let's go and consult."

He continues, "The whole group of elders would split into several small groups. They would argue among themselves and once they were through, they will all regroup again and air their support for or against a certain nominee."

The process of vetting requires that the one to be selected must not have committed any form of criminal activity such as murder. Just as our new constitution envisage a leader who will not bring any disrepute to the office, the Maa culture would not accept anyone with criminal record to be a leader.

Mzee Robert Masikonte of Enabelibel location tells me that the leader to be chosen must not have showed any characteristics of cowardice at all. "He must be valorous for him to be considered. He must not have committed sexual immorality. He must be devoid of any form of corruption" he adds.

The responsibility bestowed upon such a leader is immense and the holder would be a man of many firsts. He is the one who would be the first to be shaved as they prepare to be junior elders. He would also be the first to eat meat seen by the women, the first to marry and even the first to settle in a homestead.

Rempeyian Murasimi says, "Should there be a curse to the group of morans the selected leader was leading due to its failure to protect the community during his tenure then he will also be the first to be cursed."

Once the vetting process is complete the individual selected is taken to the *Laibon* to be appointed and approved just as the names of nominees by parliament would be forwarded to the president for appointment. Note that the agreement is entirely by consensus and no voting took place. The *Laibon* would then bless the chosen leader to begin his leadership of his generation all through his life.

It is important to note that the *Laibon* being a paramount leader, a religious leader and a seer was highly respected and, in some cases, he would reject the nominee just as the president would reject the list given to him. The whole process had to begin again.

Lelian Maasinta tells me, "The *Laibon* being a seer has the ability to see the future and he could visualize that the chosen leader could possibly cause bloodshed during his leadership. It is at this point that he will reject the nominee with very valid and concrete reasons."

If the nominee is appointed by the *Laibon* then the leader has to appreciate that he has been appointed to a position for life and that there are no monetary benefits attached to his leadership.

I ask what then are the benefit of being a Maa leader to which Maasinta says, "Being a position which involves management of relationships within and without the community such as issues to do with customs, politics, conflict resolution and many other traditional issues the leader always be respected and have the prestige associated with such an office."

Chapter Twelve

AGE-SETS AS ESSENTIAL MILESTONES IN THE MAASAI SOCIAL –POLITICAL STRATA

In the Maa male-dominated society, three major age-based male groups are recognized, namely boys, warriors (Morans) and elders. All the three groups are further stratified as junior and seniors for morans and elders and "big" and "small" for boys. Age therefore determines one's status and standing in the community. For instance, a boy would develop from a minor, almost always unnoticed and always struggling to ward off bad jokes about him, to graduate into a moran, an always fated, care-free individual who is highly visible, recognized and admired by all and very self-opinionated to eventually retire into an elder, respectable home owner cattle rearer and a member of the coveted and respected council of elders.

As part of their training at the age of 8-15 years the uncircumcised boys known as *ilayiok* spend much of their time herding their parents' cattle at this time, they imitate the behavior of the morans and develop close male relationship with their peers, that world last throughout their lives. At the end, on receiving a special signal from the elders, that the reigning morans were about to retire and it was time for a new age group to be circumcised the boys gather in large groups to begin a ceremonial dance called *enkipaata*, signaling the commencement of a new circumcision group called *Olporror*.

Mzee Stanly Ole Parit says, "When the circumcision period commences, the boys are circumcised together in a ritual that marks their transition to their new and highly coveted status as morans or warriors. Their new status is the most privileged. They roam the country side and are fed meat and milk by society and in return they defend the people and cattle against predictors and rustlers."

When the morans are not eating meat in their hideouts in the forest, they live in a warrior village specially built for them called *emanyatta*. This is an ideal cultural village where the moran learn to live in closed-knit fraternity among themselves, where all things are shared amongst themselves. For instance, no individual moran is allowed to walk alone, drink milk or even water alone.

Frank Ole Kibelekenya notes, "This restriction in their behavior kept them in each other's company, reinforcing their dependence on one another during the entire period of moranship. And this in the essence of moranship: creating a distinct age group that grows together are acts in tandem as directed by their chief moran called *Olaigwanani*. This age group is called *Olporror*."

The most distinctive feature of the Maasai society is this age group system. Two successive circumcision groups (*ilporrori*) are each stratified as either left-hand group or right-hand group. The first to be circumcised is called the right-hand group and the follower is called the left-hand group. When the two groups retire to become elders, they are paired and merged to become an age-set and given a unified name e.g *Ilkamaniki* and *Ilkalikal* become *ilnyangusi* when they were united to form an age-set.

Author H.R. Ole Kulet explains, "Authority within the age set system resides in the mentoring and in the linkage of alternating age sets in order to ensure continuity of cultural knowledge and handing down the system of power. In normal circumstances two succession circumcision groups, the left hand and the right-hand circumcision groups are in constant competition, the juniors group trying to push the reigning group out of their privileged position of moranship so that they could take over. Because of this seeming bad blood between the two groups, the mentoring responsibility for the left-hand group is not given to the right-hand circumcision group. This mentoring responsibility that is called kindling of the fire (*olpiron*) is handed to an earlier age set so that the right-hand circumcision group of the earlier age set kindles fire for the left-hand circumcision group of the latter age set and vice versa. This dual system of mentorship removes hostility of successive age groups and establishes the authority of the age set system."

In Maasai, elders collectively wield power and exercise social control over the entire community. The older the age set the more power it yields. Such power rests in the belief that elders have the power to bless and the power to curse.

In the entire age set system of empowerment young Maasai boys go through three interrelated rites of passage together from being children to being morans, then adults and finally becoming elders.

Enkipaata is a circumcision rite ushering boys into the first stage of moranhood. Eight years or so later, *Eunoto* marks the passage from moranhood to young elders and adoption of adult responsibilities, *Olngesher* marks the end of a junior elder status, the men having gone through a period apprenticeship given by senior elders and beginning the adoption of the heavy responsibilities of an elder, father and shouldering in association of age set mates, the judicial responsibilities of the society.

Chapter Thirteen

THE MAASAI SECTIONS, CLANS AND MOIETIE

The Maasai are predominantly nomadic pastoralists whose herds of cattle, sheep and goats are a common sight in the areas they occupy such as the Southern part of Kenya and the Northern districts of Tanzania.

Maasai refers to all the speakers of Maa language. The Maasai community is mainly divided into two major dialects which are the Northern and Southern Maasai.

The Northern Maa speaking community include; the *Ilsampur* who are largely known as the Samburu and the *Ilchamus* mainly found in Baringo and mainly known as the Njemps.

The Njemps are irrigation farmers and the only fishing Maasai community according to Nasieku Tarayia.

The Southern Maasai include the *Ilarusha, Ilmoitanik, Ilsiria, Ilwuasinkishu, Ilpurko, Ilkeekonyikie, Ildamat, Iloitai, Ilsikirari, Iloodokilani, Ildalalekutuk, Ilkaputiei, Ilmatapato, ilkisonko, Ilaitayiok* and *Ilparakuyo.*

According to educationist Frank Ole Kibelekenya all the above-mentioned sections of the Maasai are known in Maa as *Olosho* (Iloshon in plural). Any Maasai is primary identified with his *Olosho* or section, he adds.

He explains further that the *Iloshon* are Maasai sub tribes with a unified political and administrative structure and that each of the *Olosho* is politically autonomous.

Despite all these sections among the Maasai, the Maa community remains united by its shared culture, language and social structures.

Most of this *iloshon* constitute the Kenyan Maasai with exception of the *Ilarusha, Ilparakuo* and *Ilkisonko* who constitute Tanzania Maasai.

Robert Ole Masikonte notes that the Maasai community is further divided into clans whose members are from the same male ancestor. A clan among the Maasai is seen as a group of people who recognize descent from the same male ancestor.

The Maasai community is known to be patrilineal in that a child belongs to the clan of his father and will remain a member of the clan for life.

He explains that there are five major clans among the Maa community each with a different male ancestor.

The founding father of all the Maasai was known as Maasinta. He was also known as Leeyo. He had two wives. The first wife lived on the right hand of the gate post known in Maasai as *entailoshi e tatene*.

In the Maa community, the first wife was normally placed at the right hand gate-post while the second one was placed at the left-hand gate post at the Manyatta enclosure. The first wife had cattle that were all red in color. That's why her house was called "the one of which the calves and oxen are red", in Maa *Odomongi*.

This wife gave birth to three sons namely Lolkesen, Lelian and Losero. These three sons are the descendants of *Il-makesen* (of baboon), *Il-molelian* (of elephants) and *Il-taarosero* (of the hyena) clans respectively, which are together known as *Odomongi*.

The second wife lived on the left-hand gatepost known as *entailoishi e kidienye*. She had calves and oxen that were black in colour. Her house called "the one of which the calves and oxen are black" in Maa *Orokiteng*.

This wife gave birth to two sons namely Lukum and Naiser. These two sons are the descendants of *Il-lukumai* and *Il-laiser* clans which are represented by raven and rhinoceros respectively. Together *Il-lukumai* and *Il-laiser* are known as *Orokiteng.*

The five sons are the founding fathers of the five major clans in Maasai society.

Clans are very important among the Maasai as clan mates have a very strong communal support obligation. Clan members normally have the same branding of their cattle. Clans too have a very important role in the political system.

Clans are known as in Maasai as *Olgilata* (*ilgilat* in plural). The clans are divided in two moieties i.e. *Odomongi* - the house of the red oxen and *Orokiteng* - the house of the black cattle. Clans' members help each other in settlement of disputes, marriage including negotiations and obtaining bride-price.

Novelist H.R. Ole Kulet says, "A close observer of the Maa society would note the close-knit interdependence of the sections (*iloshon*) which doubtlessly was brought about by the survival needs of a people that lived in constant conflicts in a hostile environment. Droughts, animal diseases, cattle rustling and perpetual wildlife-human conflicts could not allow a single family the luxury of living a solitary life, hence the need for pooling resources together as clans and *iloshon* to guarantee continuity of life.

Chapter Fourteen

SOME MEDICINAL PLANTS USED BY THE MAASAI COMMUNITY

The Maasai have medicine in herbal form that is capable of curing nearly all of the diseases that affect them. The Maasai concept of medicine is not based on thousands of chemically analyzed herb samples, but rather has developed through generations of informal empirical learning and has been transmitted through a strong oral tradition.

Some of the medicines commonly used include; Olmisigiyoi (*Rhus natalensis*). It is a shrub; bark of the branchlets greyish or white and older ones dull grey, lenticillate and rough. The branchlets of this tree are used as toothbrushes. Root decoctions are taken orally to stop diarrhea. Branch decoctions administered orally for stomach upset. Leaves used in treating coughs and stomachaches. The root decoction also forms part of a medicine for hookworms. The leaf infusion is used in preparing a cough mixture.

Enkamuriaki (*Carissa edulis*) this is the Loliondo wander drug. A miracle traditional medicine believed to cure cronic diseases such as Cancer, HIV Aids, Alcers Diabetes and many more, has led to the once-dormant Loliondo Samunge village in Ngorongoro distric 400km from Arusha to turn out to be the host to thousands of people, all seeking the said miracle cure administered by a retired pastor, Mr Ambilikile Mwasapile It is a spiny, much branched, small tree, shrub with a milky sap. Roots contain an active ingredient, carissin, that may prove useful in the treatment of cancer. The twigs contain quebrachytol and cardioglycosides that are useful as an anthelmintic against tapeworm. In Maasai land root scrapings are used for glandular inflammation; ground-up roots are used as a remedy for venereal diseases, to restore virility, to treat gastric ulcers, cause abortion, and as an expectorant. An infusion of roots along with other medicinal plants is used for treating chest pains, and a root decoction is also used for treating malaria.

Osokoni (*Warburgia ugandensis*) is a spreading evergreen tree, bark smooth or scaly, pale green or brown, slash pink; bole short and clear of branches; crown rounded. Dried bark is commonly chewed and the juice swallowed as a remedy for stomach-ache, constipation, toothache, cough, fever, muscle pains, weak joints and general body pains. It is also effective in powdered form for treating the same diseases. Fresh roots are boiled and mixed with soup for the prevention of diarrhea.

Leaf decoction baths are used as a cure for several skin diseases. The inner bark is reddish, bitter and peppery and has a variety of applications. It provides treatment for the common cold; dried and ground to a snuff it is used to clear sinuses; and it is chewed, or smoke from the burning bark inhaled, as a remedy for chest complaints. The bark, roots or leaves can be boiled in water and the decoction drunk to treat malaria, but this causes violent vomiting.

Oleparmunyo (*Toddalia asiatica*). This woody liana can reach a height of up to 12m in forests as it uses other trees for support. The attractive shiny trifoliate leaves are light to dark green and are extremely aromatic, smelling of lemon when crushed. The twigs are covered in small, recurved thorns. The fruit is used by the Massai as a cough remedy and the roots in the treatment of indigestion and influenza. The leaves are used for lung diseases and rheumatism.

Olmaroroi (*Combretum molle*) is a shrub or small, graceful, deciduous tree; trunk crooked or leaning, occasionally swollen at the base. The bark is grey and smooth when young, grey-brown to almost black, rough and flaking when older, twigs often with reddish hairs. Boiled root decoction is used by the Maasai to treat stomach pains, fever, dysentery, general pains, and swellings and as an anthelmintic for hookworm. The root and leaf together are believed to be an antidote for snake bite; the juice from the leaves are drunk for chest complaints. A concoction of the inner bark is taken orally or as an enema to relieve various stomach ailments. The bark displays a gum that can be used to treat wounds, or crushed dried or fresh leaves can be used for the same purpose.

These are some of the medicines used by the Maa community.

Chapter Fifteen

THE MAASAI DIET

According to the World Health Organization (WHO) nutrition is the intake of food, considered in relation to the body's dietary needs. Good nutrition - an adequate, well balanced diet combined with regular physical activity - is a cornerstone of good health. Poor nutrition can lead to reduced immunity, increased susceptibility to diseases, impaired physical and mental development and reduced productivity.

Over the years the Maasai community has been relying on meat, milk and blood from their cattle for protein and energy needs. Meat was and still is one of the most important sources of energy and protein. Contrary to the belief that Maasai eat meat daily the Maasai only consumed meat during special occasions such as circumcision, marriage ceremonies and on major family or community events.

Mzee Johan Kasura explains, "Because meat is shared freely among family members and with others who may visit when an animal has been slaughtered, chances are that there will always be a family that has slaughtered and meat is available in many homesteads on a given day".

Some of the ceremonies where meat is consumed according to him include; *Enkino-sata oo nkiri* (the eating of the meat ceremony) also known as *Olngesher* in Maa, *Olkiteng loo lbaa* or the ox of the wounds, *enkiyama* - marriage, *Olkiteng loo nkulalen* or the ox of the ear-plugs, *olkiteng loo lkuiyanat* or the ox of the patterns just to mention but a few.

The meat was in most cases roasted over charcoal or the embers of a fire. There were some parts of the meat that were strictly meant for women as some were for men.

Occasionally meat and bones were boiled to get soups. The soups were blended with herbs which had medicinal value.

Osarge which is the Maasai word for blood, was and is still an essential part of the Maa nutrition. When you visit a Maasai village or homestead you will probably see young Maasai warriors wrestle with a struggling cow while another patiently waits with his bow drawn, arrow ready to strike. Once the animal is held in the right position the warrior with the arrow head shoots straight at the bovine's jugular. Warm blood gushes out into a waiting guard.

Once the guard is almost filled, the punctured neck is sealed with a blob of cow dung then the cow is released. This is how the Maasai get the blood they use in their diet. However, Robert Masikonte of Enaibelibel location in Narok county notes that getting blood from cattle was restricted only to the time of a biting drought when there was very little milk or any other food for the family. At a time like this he explains that the drawn blood was mixed with milk to make a nutritious drink called *Osaroi,* that was given to the family members and especially the young children.

The Maa people drink blood ritually and for refreshment in its pure form. Blood is a good source of iron and calcium. They believe blood makes them very strong.

The main source of blood that the Maa people drink according to Walter Kiranto of Eor-enkitok village in Narok; is from the slaughtered animals. And because animals are slaughtered often to mark an occasion, blood was always availed at the onset of a ceremony.

Unlike milk, blood was not used a blessing or curse but had several special instances where it was used.

Frank Ole Kibelekenya, "After giving birth for instance, the woman took *Osarge.* If the baby was a boy the blood she took was from a bull and if it was a girl the blood she took was from a heifer. During circumcision ceremonies when boys officially became warriors, an age-set, leader known as *Ol-aiguenani* who was selected among the initiates, would be the first to drink the warm blood of the slaughtered animal. That was ritually an indication of the leadership status of the individual attained in his age-group".

During *Eunoto* ceremony which is a graduation of the morans to junior elders' status the leader of the group also led the rest in the drinking of the blood from the bulls' jugular vein. Blood was also given to a member of the family who lost blood through an injury or debilitating sickness.

Milk was and still is the most important component of the Maasai diet. Unlike meat and blood which are consumed occasionally milk was consumed daily.

Generally stored and carried in long, decorated guards which were washed with urine that acted as mild antiseptic and dried using an aromatic burning ember made from the sacred *Oloirien* splinters. Milk and its products were consumed by all regardless of their age. The milk was either fresh from the cow and ingested without being boiled, sour milk known in Maa as *Kule naisamis* which was made by fermenting the fresh milk for a day at room temperature, or yoghurt known as *kule naoto* - milk that was fermented for several days in an airtight container. And finally cow colostrum known as *isikitok* - when it was still thick and yellow in colour it was considered nutritious and mostly given to young children.

Milk was considered a gift from *Enkai Narok*, had deep, symbolic importance as it was believed to have spiritual properties and that was why it was used on several rituals among the Maasai.

Embolosat ceremony is one of the rituals where milk was used. This was a ceremony which ushered in the period of early manhood.

Another ceremony where milk as used was *Eokoto e-kule* or the milk drinking ceremony.

Chapter Sixteen

MAASAI AND THEIR CATTLE ARE INSEPARABLE

The Maasai are widely known to uphold the culture of pastoralism. Though there some sections of the Maa which practice agriculture such as *il-arusha* found mainly in Arusha Tanzania and even those who rely on fishing such as *il-tiamus* found in Baringo Central and North near Lake Baringo still most of the Maasai's are pastoralists. The hallmark of pastoralism is mainly Cattle rearing. So, in the life of a Maasai cattle are very important and any attempt to restrict the Maasai from this cultural practice is tantamount to destroying the fundamentals of the community's survival.

The Maasai's have over the years developed a kind of a magical relationship with cattle especially the cows. There is an inherent believe among the community that *Enkai–* the God of the Maa gave the community the cattle for safe keeping and this has somehow justified their raiding of other communities' cattle. The Maa community loves their cattle so much and hence the life of any Maasai revolves around the cattle that is why nearly all roles and social status are entirely derived from the individual's relationship with the cattle.

Mzee Johnah Kasura, "The cattle mean a lot to the community; they are a source of food in form of milk and meat. Traditionally the Maa community does not grow crops or even do hunting. Their way of life has always been through herds of cattle".

He noted the Maa community does not eat meat wild animals and that's why they do not hunt, anyone who hunts and ate wild animals' meat was regarded as *oltoroboni* meaning a poor man.

Susan Noonkipa of Eor-ekule says, "We make our mattress, shoes and many other accessories using hide from cattle. We also use it to decorate the milk guards and making belts". Among the Maasai community it is the women who made or built houses and the dung of the cattle again played an important role as it was used to plaster and to do the decoration of the house.

Elizabeth Naneu notes that, "Their dung comes in handy when it comes to plastering our huts and also making decorative patterns on them". The cattle are a major sign of wealth. To the Maasai the more the cattle you had the richer and highly regarded in the society you were. Cattle has for years been used by the community as a currency for trade. They have been used to pay for brides and for building relationships. They have also been used to pay for the fines when one was convicted of a criminal offence. Today they are used to pay for school fees of many young Maasai kids.

Malit Ole kabelekenya, "Cattle have everything we need as a community. They symbolize our wealth and are a source of pride to us since our lives revolves around them". He notes that cattle are used to build lasting relationships between families known as *Enkaputi.*

Assuming that the marriage proposal is acceptable and *Enkaputi* is established, MzeeKasura notes "The bridegroom on the wedding day brings two heifers and one bull, all of which ought to be of the same colour and blameless with no scars. He also brings two female sheep, a ram and a lamb. Of the heifers brought by the young man one is given to the girl's father so that there after the young man and his father-in-law will call each other 'Pa-kiteng' or 'En-tawuo'while the lamb is given to the bridegroom's mother-in-law and henceforth the young man and his age set call her 'Pa-ker' meaning the one whom I gave a lamb."

They cattle were socially used to create and strengthen ties and loyalties among the community. They were used for payment of fines which re-establishes social cohesiveness that had been eroded due to one reason or another.

Maasai tend to give each other presents of cattle, sheep and goats depending on family ties and relationships. The donor and receipt will henceforth call each other by the name of the cattle. That's why you will hear the Maasai calling each other such names as *Pa-kiteng!* Meaning "O giver of cow!" *En-tawuo!* Meaning "O giver of heifer!" *Pa-ker!* "O giver of sheep!" *Pa – kine!* "O giver of goat!". This is how much the life of the Maasai is entwined by the cattle they keep. The closeness is so strong that even during drought the Maa would never sell their cattle.

Peter Koyiara says, "We are not going to sell our cattle just because there is drought. If they die, let them die and what remains is what God found fit to be ours" He notes that cattle's have also been used in almost all Maasai ceremonies from *Einoto* (birth) to *En-keeya* (death). When the Maa community wanted to appease God due to human faults they would sacrifice by slaughtering of a holy sheep; cow or goat in a ceremony known as *Empolosare*. Another ceremony is known as *Enkibung'ata e mowuo O lkiteng* meaning the ceremony of holding the Ox's horns which is a purification ceremony where by all one's sins are forgiven and is also known as *Olkiteng' Loo Ibaa.*

Here Robert Ole Masikonte of Enaibelibel location in Narok explains further about the ceremonies. *Ol-kiteng loo lbaa*, the ox of the wounds; this he notes was a cleansing ceremony where by elders of the same age set - *Olporror* would come together and slaughter an ox in order to repent all the sins they did during their term as morans. It was basically cleaning themselves from the wounds of the past so as to bring peace in their old age.

He continues; "Other ceremonies included *o-lamal*, the delegation, *e-murata oo nkera*, the circumcision of his children, and attending *em-polosare oo nkera*, a sacrifice for his children whereby one would slaughter an ox as a sacrifice in dedication of his children to *Enk-ai* in presence of elders of his age set and *Oloibon*."

Despite all these entwinements, the culture of cattle rearing especially in large numbers is currently not making economic sense hence the community needs to think of a change of strategy-a kind of a paradigm shift.

Mzee John Ole Koonyo advices, "The community has been moving from place to place in search of green pastures for many years and it's now high time it settled and engage itself in a more economically sound activity. Many factors which include erratic weather pattern; frequent droughts and floods have made our herds to vanish year after year leaving us in abject poverty.

Let the community think of investing in education; real estate; stock market; modern agriculture through the use of green houses and also in many other viable businesses".

Chapter Seventeen

GOD, DEATH AND INHERITANCE AMONG THE MAASAI COMMUNITY

The Maasai are spiritual people who believe in a God known as Enk-ai. The Maasai God is renowned as a creator of the forests, mountains, plains and highlands. Enk-ai is highly respected and is prayed to by all in the Maasai community. It is this God that the Maa inherently believe gave them cattle for safe keeping. The God is believed to dwell not only in the heavens but also in the thick forests, rivers and beneath the earth. This explains the spiritual significance the Maa community attaches to forests especially the Mau and Naimina Enkiyio forests which forms the basis of its very livelihood.

The Maasai believe in one God who has dualistic distinctiveness which are contrasting to each other. *Enk-ai Na-rok-*the god which is black, the good, generous and benevolent god; personified by wind and rain, and *Enk-ai Na-nyokie-*the red god, the bad or revenging god the master of life and death; personified by thunder and lightning.

So, when *Enk-ai Na-nyokie* strikes and there is death in a Maa family, the entire community is affected. Death is really dreaded among the Maa community and its occurrence brings along a sorrowful dark cloud that envelops all those who hear of it. There are no elaborate mortuary practices among the Maasai and no beliefs in life after death. The Maa people believe that once life has come out of the body, the body has no use anymore and that's why they do not bury the dead but rather throw them away in the forest to be devoured by wild animals. In fact, in some occasions the dead would be smeared with fat so that they could easily attract wild animals devour the bodies.

Known as *En-keeya* in Maasai language death was one thing no Maasai wanted to encounter. This fear of death made some in the community when they suspected that one of their own was about to die and had no chance of surviving, to take him or her away from their enkang' and would tie a string on one of the victim's big toes which they would occasionally pull to see if he or she was alive. When they pulled the string and the person responded then they knew he or she was alive. If they pulled again and there was no response then they knew that the individual was dead.

When a person died at the homestead-enkang' the Maasai would vacate that house-enkaji and move to another one. They would pay a man who had no family known in Maa as Olkirikoi to remove the dead, smear it with fat and take it for disposal in the forest. For a woman, life ended with death, but for the man after death, there was En-jung'ore or En-jung'go. This is inheritance.

According to mzee Johnmark Kamakei of Olchurai in Gilgil, inheritance among the Maasai is a very important process which begins when an old man becomes conscious that he is about to die or when sudden death of an old man occurs.

"Once an old man realizes that he is soon going to die he bequeaths his properties to all his sons. It is also at this point in time that he will also appoint the son who will inherit his debts," he adds.

The other instance where the process of inheritance would be initiated, he tells me is when there was sudden death of an old man. In case of such unexpected death of the old man either due to diseases or war, his eldest son would inherit both his father's properties and debts. To signify his important position as the new head of the home after the departure of the father, this son wears a bracelet called Ol-kataar.

Frank Ole Kibelekenya says "The eldest son who inherits his father's property due to his unanticipated death is supposed to share out both the properties and the debts among his younger brothers including the step-brothers."

The men hold and control the main types of properties namely land and livestock while women generally own household goods and only have rights to use land and livestock. The girl child or daughters in Maa culture do not inherit properties. She only enjoys symbolic ownership of the cattle identified with her at the family estate. But as soon as she gets married, she loses this claim. However according to Nasieku Tarayia an old man has authority and exclusive right to apportion her anything in his estate as he is the final arbiter and no one would risk to go against his wish lest a curse befalls him.

There are scenarios whereby a father may have fathered only girls. In such a situation, Robert Ole Masikonte says, "The old man is expected to prevent one of his daughters from getting married. The young woman was then authorized to have children at her father's home with any man of her choice. In case she got a baby boy then it was pronounced the heir of the old man's property." Such scenarios are rare as the Maasai being polygamous, would in one way or another have one of the kids being a son.

According to Nasieku Tarayia no one in the traditional Maasai society was to inherit land. He notes that livestock is the actual property to be inherited and shared in the Maasai traditional society.

Disputes would always arise on how the distribution of the property should be done. In such a case Ole Masikonte notes that it is purely the duty of the elders within the community to resolve the impasse.

Chapter Eighteen

MAASAI HERITAGE TO KENYA

The Maasai community is largely a pastoralist community which keeps on moving from place to place in search of greener pasture. As the Maasai's moved from one place to another they kept naming the places they been through in their search for pastures for their cattle which meant everything to them. The naming was done according to the rivers they came across; according to the waters they encountered; according to trees, shrubs, creepers, weeds and the list is endless.

If you have been to Nairobi you probably know Buruburu, Lang'ata, Dagoretti and Embakasi. You probably do not have any idea that all these names have their origin to the Maa language. To begin with Nairobi itself which is our capital city; the name Nairobi comes from the name the Maasai gave to the waters of Nairobi river- *Enkare Na-irobi* meaning the water which is cold. Buruburu is another part of Nairobi that got its name from the Maasai. In Maa it's known as *Em-pulpul* which means a Low laying land where water can gather and stay a kind of depression. Lang'ata known in Maa as *E-lang'ta* means a river crossing. It is in such river crossing that lovers used to meet in those days and that's why a girlfriend is known as *e-lang'ata*to date in Maasai dialect. Dagoretti known in Maa as *En-daguretti* is a wild plant known scientifically as *Gomphocarpus physcocarpus*. Empakasi is a name of a small river.

As you drive towards Narok from Nairobi you come across a place called Kijabe just before you get to Mai Mahihu town. This place is mostly known for its missionary hospital that has for many years treated thousands and thousands of patients. It is one hospital that is really loved and cherished by the Maa community for it has given them service for years and years. This place has very cold winds which the Maa call *En-kijabe* and hence the name Kijabe.

Moving from Mai Mahihu to Naivasha the Maasai saw a pool of water to which they called *E-naiposha* hence the name Naivasha. A few miles from this pool of water is a Mountain with valleys in it known in Maasai language as *O-loo-nong'ot* meaning that it is of the valleys. Today this mountain is known as Mt. Longonot. Still moving towards Nakuru you meet a bush of *Acacia pennata*– this bush is known by the Maasai as *Ol-girigiri* and the name has since been corrupted to Gilgil.

From Gilgil the next town you meet is a town that used to be bare, grassless and dusty area known in Maasai as *E-nakurro.* The place is today known as Nakuru Town. Between Gilgil and Nakuru is a small centre named by the Maasai after a creeper plant known as *Ol-muteita.* This creeper plant was found in Elementaita in plenty and that's why the place is nowadays corruptly called Elemetaita.

Most of you might not know that Njoro derived its name from the Maa *Ol-chorro* which means a spring of water. Londiani is a corrupted version of *Loo-ntiyan* meaning it is of the bamboo's or *En-tiyiani* that is small bamboos.

The list long and almost endless but before I pen off there are two names that the Maasai gave to the Kamba towns in a rather interesting way. This first one is Makueni. As you know the Maasai's and

Kamba's have a long history due to their neighborliness. So, at one time the Maasai man will tell the Kamba counterpart "I am not Laughing!" in Maa *Makwen* and the Kamba would hear Makueni and since then the area has been known as Makueni. The second name is Kilome. While fighting with the Kamba's the Maasai's on the other side of the hill they sow arrows coming over the hills to their side and could not see who was throwing them they lamented *Kilome!* Meaning a bad thing and so the place is now known as Kilome. That's Maasai heritage to Kenya.

THE END

Made in United States
North Haven, CT
05 September 2022

23703012R00082